TILL THE END

(A Collection of poems)

Deporah Zoe S Staji

AELAY PUBLISH

Till the End - Poetry
All CopyRights Reserved By © Deporah Zoe S Staji 2021
Author: Deporah Zoe S Staji
First Edition: Augest 2021

Published By:
Aelay Publish
5/175, Fathima nagar,
Kuthenkuly,
Tirunelveli -627104
Phone: 9944992571

Design And Executed by

ISBN : 978-93-5533-195-3
Page : 83

ACKNOWLEDGEMENTS

This work is imperfect but the love and support given during the journey finishing it are honest. It is not merely about the result, but the process. I worship Thee, the Almighty Jesus Christ, to whom I walk with, for His undemanding love, for always waiting for me whenever I run out from Him and get lost

I would like to thank my beloved father, Stanly, for supporting me in his unique ways and my loving mom, Jasmin J Shiji for love, prayers and patient in every 'evil' thing I do. I thank my younger brother, Stajin for big love, laugh and hug.

I would like to thank my supporting pillars Viola, Kavi Nilavoo, Sureha, Georsha, Nandhitha & Monish I'll forever be grateful for the encouragement you all gave me when I needed it.

Till the End

I would like to thank my mentors Dr. P. Jeyappriya, Dr. A. Muthu Meenalosini & Dr. S. Peter Samuel, your encouragement; love and support have been invaluable.

I would like to thank my Instagram family (@bees_life11) Words can't express how much I appreciate your support and motivation.

I would like to thank EVERYONE who ever said anything positive to me or taught me something. I heard it all, and it meant something.

Last but not least, I would like to thank fidzgk, for inspiring me to write poetry.
I am thankful to you readers for accepting my first book.

Dearest Amma...

Life is better when you're next to me and I thank you for making me who I am today, thanks for leading me in paths of good and for teaching me everything I need to be happy.

I carry you in my heart and I will continue doing it forever. Your memory always fills me with joy and gives me peace of mind.

There's no bond quite like that between mother and child. You know me in ways no one else ever will. You also see in me all the things I can still become and continue having faith that I can do and be whatever I want, no matter what my age. You are my biggest fan, my mentor, my confidant, my hero, my turn-to person when my world comes crashing down and the first person I call to tell when things are going great. The comfort that comes from our friendship, the confidence that your faith in me instils, and your unquestioning support of whatever I do, is irreplaceable.

The kind of there-for-me that you are is the very essence of what makes a great mother. I wear your unconditional love and support around me like a big hug every single day.

I am so blessed to have you in my life. I've probably said it before — you are my angel on earth. Thank you for always, always being at my side and having my back. No one is in my corner quite the way you are. I treasure you, mumma, and love you more than life itself. You are an amazing soul ever ready to learn something new, always open to differing opinions, and so compassionate and kind. You have always taught by example. There'll never be a day in my life when I won't need you.

Love you to infinity & beyond!!

PSALM

As the light showeth on her face

She stills, and fixes her gaze;

Something or someone; somehow

Got her mind saying "wow"

But as the illuminated haze increaseth, her

Expressions calm, she picks up the Bible

and turns to a Psalm

POETRY WILL KEEP ME ALIVE..!

and I hope poetry will keep me alive

and I hope my words won't die when I die

I regret nothing

But I wouldn't want to live a life

that ends when I die

I know hearts that read my poetry

will carry me

I know eyes that see my light

will remember me

I know the sun won't forget me

and sky will forever know me

Cause I am more than a human

I am a star on land

for the stars of sky

to look down and smile at

and maybe you are too.

MY LOVING BROTHER

You are the one, I grew up with
You are the one, I played along
You are the one, I admired the world with
You are the one, my whole life revolved
You are the one, I enjoyed each day with
You are the one, I shared my secrets with
You are the one, I stated as my saviour
You are the one, my enthusiasm lasted long with
You are the one, I welcome each moment with smile
You are the one, I feel close by even when distance parts us
You are the one, I miss so much even when, we converse
with
You are the one, my dear brother, I wish always to be,
reborn with!

EVERYTHING...

Recently, I noticed that everything!
Everything "we have"
becomes "we had"
Everything changes with time
so do people
It's too priority to know
your value in their life
before making them
your happiness;
It's too priority to make
yourself prior before making
anyone else,
It's too priority to fall in love with
yourself than with someone else
People you care,
will care for someone else
People you love,
will love someone else
And that's not you are worth of
Leave someone who treats
You like the rest in their life
Because not every diamonds
Belongs to your life!

MINE EVER

Dad is someone who grasps me when I weep

Berates me when I smash the rules

Shimmers with delight when I prosper and

Has confidence in me even when I fail

Behind every happy girl, there is a soul

Called dad;

Only men who never hurts

With smile and love cures everything

Day when I saw him in tears is the day

Stopped to hurt him

Love you wholeheartedly.

A FEW THINGS

A few things
That brings me
Delight when I am
Depressed;
I pen my notepad
I watch my favourite cartoons
Or read a book;
Play games
Or eat some frozen food;
Music make better
A few things which
I can enjoy alone
Few things that
Matter to me
And they always bring
a twinkle on my face
Even if I weep in the bathroom
Even if I had an awful day
Even if I feel nothing
Even if my mood is terrible
Even if people stab me
Or throw me out
These few things always
Make me peace!

Deporah Zoe S Staji

TAKE ME AWAY!

Take me away!
Take my heart,
I will give it with ease
Take my hand and walk
This journey with me
Take these scars
And heal them all up
Take these fears
And make them vanish,
When things get tough
Take this smile and
Make it stretch so wide
Take these arms and
Hold me on so tight
Take these feelings and
Make them real
At the end, show me
How to feel.
Take me away!
Take me to the beach,
I can see a beautiful creature
Swimming around joyful
Take me to the jungle,
I can hear the most beautiful
Voice singing and the cold wind
Take me to the top of mountains,

Till the End

It's just I see the whole world
Take me to the place,
Where I can be away from
Ignorance, pain, fakeness
And hurt;
Take me to the place,
Where promises are valued
Take me to the place,
Where there is no struggle,
No uncertainty and no fear;
Take me away;
Far, far, far away!

TIME

Walking with a faded pain,
I hobble every next, for delight.
No faith, no belief, not even
greed, in my losing stride.

Wasted for good, wasted by glory,
I delve for an emotion.
Slapped by destiny, swindled by time
Sensing a foreboding

Well, the times shall change,
the times shall sail.
But the love, for a soul that blessed
my world, shall never ever fail.

WAVES...

My soul is like an ocean
A spot of untold worries,
My soul is like an ocean
With waves of misery and
anxiety forever popping in;
These waves are getting
heavy and heavy to elude
These waves are getting
sturdy and sturdy
each break
These waves are pulling
me under further and
further every day
These waves are consuming
me at a concerning step
It's time to let these waves
pull me to a better place.
Waves ceaselessly wash
away footmark,
like time cleanse away,
leaving you with an onset.
Waves wash away
the good and bad.
Time and waves don't
discriminate.

All circumscribe,
Everything returns to
the open sea.
It's just a matter of time
Before you're washed away.

you can be wonderful as a sea
but not everyone will like you
Some will avoid you
Some will fear you
Some will look for you
and some others
will dream of you

After the storms I went through,
My soul knew no strength
Amidst an ocean of tears
Floated my weighless body
Carried by the waves of death
My heart, however, hummed prayers
For an unexpected miracle
Pushing me to the shores
Where lies my peace of mind!

IT WON'T..

To naively trust someone and

show them your weakest spots

is like giving guns to the enemies

and hope they will not fire,

It's like throwing punches in the mirror

praying that your knuckles won't bleed

It's like talking to the sky

thinking it will understand

and eventually talk back

but, "IT WON'T...!!"

SELF LOVE

They say,

wait for the right person

to come, to love & to heal

your broken pieces

But,

I just ask, why?

Why does it have to be

another person?

Why can't you, I, us

can heal and love ourselves

Why there has to be a person

and a right time?

POETRY EXIST IN MANY WAYS

There is poetry
in the way you exist

There is poetry
in the way you wake up
after a struggling night

There is poetry
in the way
you stay kind to
others & yourself

There is poetry
in the feelings
you feel but
couldn't express..

They often ask me who
this poem is about and
I have no answer
how can a
Poem describes someone
because people often
change but
poems forever remain
the same..

Till the End

It's hard to be a poet
through your poems you would be
Trying to convey your inner feelings
So that someone would come and hug you,
But all you will be getting is
Appreciation for the rhyming of some
Arranged words in a paragraph.

SILENCE IS DRIZZLE

I lost myself in the rain
Standing there soaked through
A wreckage of dreams and hopes
Washed away for something new!

What do I want?
I want books and candles.
Coffee in rain.
A hand that's warm.
Mountains and a window
to stare at them

WAITING FOR THE RAIN

I perch and gaze
as the rain slumps
from a azure so dark
and silvery

Is this life
a crying sky?
If so,
not even I can brawl.

I'm drained of hurting,
I'm tired of sobbing.
I'm sick of being alone
for all these ages.

I want serene,
and I want love.
I want to break free
to fly above!

A SMILE…

Ask me why I wear a crown
and I will show you my sword
Ask me why I wield a sword
and I will show you my scars
Ask me why I have scars
and I will show you my smile!

I am on my way to reach you
Stones blocked me in the way
I stood still cherishing the

Moments,
When you taught birds to sing
I spoke with flowers and

told them
That you're the first one

that made me
Smile!!

Till the End

Behind the flattering smile,
she has her iron strength
because Athena rests in her spirit,
she is wisdom and the art of war
that is why she wins her wars
without shedding blood.

Some people love me, some hate me.
Some encourage m , some use abusive

Words,
We all know life is a lesson.
The same person who praises us today

Will put us down one day.
But one thing which life taught me is

"Not to live for others but to

Live for God and for myself".
We are not here to please people but God.
For all these love, backstabs and hate

My response will be the same.
Yea it's just a SMILE
Never lose your smile!
It's the greatest reply you can ever give back!

PAINT YOUR OWN SKY

Pick the brush
and paint your sky
with whatever colours
you have in mind.

Blues and greens
whatever you feel
are matching
with your broken rhymes.

Don't add the greys
if they make you feel low
don't add more colours
just for the outer show.

The reds, the purples
if they cheer your heart
add them for the days
when you are falling apart.

But paint your sky
with the colours you like
paint it with
what makes you smile.

Deporah Zoe S Staji

Walk on the clouds,
swim in the rainbow,
breath in the sun rays,
fall with the raindrops,
smile at the touch of breeze,
and rest on the leaves like a dewdrop.

It's beautiful how
in such a complicated world
a single smile
can turn ashes into gold..!

It doesn't take much to
change the world
A hug here, a smile there,
A prayer here, some kindness there
You can wait for some big revolution
Or you can be someone's sunshine today.

THE LOSS IS NOT YOURS

Over and over again
Life sends you cactus'
By reminding you that
You're getting
Over attached
emotionally and
Overused
Or being taken
For granted.
And,
That's okay.
Smile and go on,
The loss is not yours.

SHE

She carry storm in her eyes,
Where thousands of thoughts reside
Is it possible to mess with that side
Where your arguments don't
even give a fight!

She has peace in her smile
where you'll find home to hide
she is chaos with terms and
conditions applied
Behave the way and she will
make everything alright.

She is a flower
holding herself together
by her roots
using every drop
of rain or tears
to make herself stronger
when she is ready
she will turn towards
the love shining on her
and open her petals
to reveal the
magnificent beauty
that she is..

BELIEVE IN YOURSELF

If you believe you can survive,
you can survive in unwanted love.
If you believe you can make it,
you will win yourself.
If you believe you have patience in you,
you are great enough to face restrictions
for you for anything you want.
But once if you stop believing yourself,
everything will be left out of hands.
If you stop believing yourself,
you'll loose everything that you have already.

TEARS AWAY

How beautiful it is to cry!
Sometimes I wonder
the tiny sour droplets
taking away burden, suffering, anguish
from our heart, through our cheeks
how peaceful it is to cry..!

Sitting near the window
crying with the moon
we confess how much
we miss each other's stars.

I was told to not hold back
my tears,
To let them flow as they are
So I'm laying here alone
Wondering if they'll ever stop!

I WONDER WHERE DO THOUGHTS GO

I wonder where do thoughts go
Do they flow with the sand
below my feet,
Rushing to elope with
the turquoise sea,
Do they sit on the petals of flowers
Blooming and resting for a little bit
Do they fly to different lands
On the feathers of birds
Do they freeze in the cold
And seek shade in the heat
Do they fall in the rain
Cocooned in little droplets
Do they slide down colourful paths
In the playground of clouds and rainbows
Do they linger on like a memory
Or do they drift with the wind
that is already carrying
Thoughts with it since centuries
I wonder where do thoughts go.

WANDERING ALONE

I'm always alone
wanted to know why?
I was so scared to lose
all the people I had
So, I pushed them away
and watched them leave
I broke my own heart
before they got a chance to!

She works alone in the sepia filled
Room of her heart listening through
The fading light to
Spidery conversations,
Sewing a seam that reveals a picture
Of fragile blood and misty sea halos,
As silence begins to invade her
Solitude she lights a candle
Which burns a
Soporific glow upon this seduction,
Her own mercurial darkness.

Till the End

Amidst the cluttered crowdy city
A deep silence was her aura,
the little girl who fell in love
with the silence of darkness
got buried under the street lights.

In a room full of people I feel
so alone
Oh! What I'd give to not feel
at all
for all emotions to be gone
But I'll still rise with the
morning sun
another night goes by
Where I wish I don't wake up.

MY ZEN

I leave this room with so many writings on the walls
If these walls could speak
They'd tell you the story of a girl who has lost
herself so many times
but something would always call her back ashore
I leave this room with an ocean of emotions
Every moment,
I wish I could've kept in a bubble for later
I'd leave this room with so many bubbles you'd drown
Days when things felt too deep
I'd crawl into my bed in this room and breath
This is my Zen..!

NEVER EVER BEG SOMEONE

never begs someone
to be with you.
Never beg for attention,
commitment, affection,
time and effort.
Never beg someone
to come back.
Never beg someone
to be in your life,
You should never have
to ask to feel wanted.
Begging is demanding
and degrading.
If someone doesn't
willingly give u these things,
with their arms wide open,
they aren't worth it.
No one, under any
Circumstances,
is ever worth begging for.

Deporah Zoe S Staji

THE SUN

She was once like the sun

Bright with all her beauty

Eager to explore the world

with all she thought it was

but went down the dark path

And witnessed the true world

With all its fancy deception

And bittersweet mockery

Yet she stands strong and proud

With scars life gifted her

For she knows who she is now

The light and dark as one

As the sun rises every day

I wished for her to stay

A little more so that I could say

As the glowing sunlight

I wished for her to be

with me every night

Till the End

A little more so that I can say

But, now I could only wish

If she could be with me

As the sun

And it's glowing light

A little more so that I could say.

You came like a sun,

Showered light to the grey

And just like how the sun

Fades out on the horizon

You took all your light away

Leaving this world darker

Then it has ever been!

YOU AND ME

You and Me – Sun
Made from stardust
You and me
You were the sun,
and I was life
I ride through the meadows
And you cleared
my path with light
I smile to you and
you shine back too
Showed me the path
to drive through
We had our time every day
Then you would send
the moon to take a break
But you came back
as the brightest day

You shined on me
till the final day
Showered me with love
and cleared my way
Never realized you would
go away forever
As we were stardust
you and me.

I EVOLVE!

There is a room at the
top of the staircase
past an Alcove;
Where the angles
once played, Here only
silence and the soft
Shifting of features
remain, There are times
when I'm nothing
And I'm able to hold
my own heart In my
hands, It is a valve
that never ceases to
spray me with the
dark foam of my blood;
In this room, all is
un-fictional In this room, I evolve!

REALITY

At the rollercoaster ride of living
when I speak about Knowledge
have you ever been so perfect?
When warmth comes nearby
why the output is religious error?
Is it about to fright?
When the two emotions are clear;
Passing critical remark Is a trend;
Have you ever been through
the same?
When I talk about fright,
All I'm talking about failure
Why to fright failure?
Isn't it letting you grow proper?
When I talk about humanity
don't show your insanity
Keep a little bit of integrity
and change this reality.

ARE YOU OKAY??

Are you okay...?
Have you been able to
sleep...?
Every night I stare at my
Phone
As it all becomes about you
Every day I continue on
Just as I did before

You always thought
I controlled you
You never believed me
When I told you
I stood my own ground
But I'll always wish every night
I could look you in the eyes
And ask you
Are you okay...?
Have you been able to sleep!!

NOBODY KNOWS

I'm jealous of those people
who end their days so well
they don't have to think twice
if they are living in hell...?
I live constantly in pain,
Always feeling agony,
I don't feel sorry for myself,
I made myself this tragedy

Every night before I sleep
I have a habit of overthinking
I shouldn't have said that
was I too much..!!
Am I really not enough..!!
These thoughts linger my mind
As I feel forgotten and left behind,
But I have no right to complain
I made my life this way!

MEMORY LANE

If you want to know
How I feel about you,
Just listen to the songs
That I made you hear,
Because the lyrics scream
All the words I can't
Seem to say
I've tried many times but
The words just won't
Escape from my lips
Whenever you're around
Those songs are
My unwritten love letter
To you, My Love!

HOPE, WILL BE YOURS!

There is no need to worry,
no need to wear yourself down
with these heavy thoughts
no point in running
and chasing what keeps slipping away
for what is yours
is already coming your way

It's time to forget
the changes around you
and focus on
what's changing in you
for all you're wishing for
will be yours
once you're ready
so let go of your desire
to control it all
and know that eventually
it will all make sense
and every missing piece
will fall into place

GLORIOUS SUNSHINE

Sometimes
there is no answer,
we just have to make
the best of what
happens to us,
walk with our heads
held high,
with confidence in our stride
and love in our hearts,
in order to have peace
of mind;
not everything can
be solved,

Not everything can
be justified,
we must face those fears,
but everything in the
end WILL be just fine.
Like there's glorious
sunshine;
after every heavy Rain
There's fruitful Reward
agree every pain and
hardship you endure!

MOMENTS IN TIME

The haunting voice of mine
is lingering in my head
Sound like an echo in a
Dark shadow;
But yet too scary besides me
I became drenched in a horror

But still, I am hidden in a
Dark shadow;
Our word is full of ghosts
Of unspoken words and memories
But still their chocking voice
Fumbled in my ears
I became shivered when I wrote these
Because I know it isn't real!!

THINGS FALL APART

What happens when
things fall apart again,
and I find myself on the floor,
all broken up and lost
ever after all this
progress?

Well,
the thing I learned from
the garden is-
I'm not at all at risk.
This is what roots are for.

ONLY YOU

You will be
weaving your heart
Mending your
Broken pieces together
& it will look
Beautiful again

Don't ask how
& Who will do
My dear it's you,
Only you!

BEE'S RHYTHMS

A heart that endured
the pain for years
is now where the kindness dwells
to heal the scars of others

Till the End

I was told to not hold back
my tears,
To let them flow as they are
So I'm laying here alone
Wondering if they'll ever stop!

When you ask me
how will I get through this
how will I find resilience to trust again
When all I see is red, how will I find softness
how will I resurface
I will say;
With time.

Because that is what women do!

Till the End

"Can I change my fate" asked the man.
"Only if you want to" answered the butterfly.

Butterfly, symbol of transformation

for all the people
that I no longer know
there's a place in my heart
that you'll forever hold,
while our time together
was temporary:
and was, so long ago
you became a part of me
that I'll never ever let go!

Till the End

The wall around my heart
grew stronger and stronger
with each loss
my suffering hardened into protection
and then softened as growth.

Each tear drop was filled
with secrets,
secrets that only it knew
And that secret hidden away
Like a memory!

Till the End

Take a leap of faith
you'll probably fall
but you'll learn how to jump
the next time you'll just jump harder!

Sitting with the sounds of silence
all I can hear
is the noise of my thoughts
weaving words play in my mind
Spilled ink to capture the rhythms.

Till the End

Our love was wild like the wind
and I'd give anything
to have my hair tangled up
in your hands again.

If I were a needle
I would stich the
old torned out
dreams that seem
hopeless today.

Till the End

I am learning to be the eye
of my hurricane.
To be the calm in my chaos
To spin and crash and break
and still be at peace..

Entangle yourself in the
embrace of your arms
once in a while,
for self love is the holy grail.

Till the End

Trust the timing
for the efforts,
the love,
the hate,
the respect
and everything
Which you have put in
will come back to you.
You'll receive it
from the universe,
as nothing here operates
one-way
you will get
all these back
Have faith!

Remember the light
inside of you
and how powerful
it can shine
given to the right hands
that know the worth
that they hold

Till the End

And I found inner peace
when I started living quietly
after I learned that
not everyone who wishes me well
truly wants the best for me.

After long tiring day,
I look at myself in the mirror
praising myself for not giving up
and realizing that the
person in the mirror loves
me so much and always
Supports, without arguing!

Till the End

You have depths that flourish in
subterranean blindness and if i took
a walk through your doorway i would
make the descent down into your heart
filling my lungs with your tattered song
for you are an arched void where
Fearless things take shelter.

You
Came like a storm
Gone like a hurricane
and blew up my sleeps
of umpteenth nights;
Very little moments with
irreplaceable memories..!!

Till the End

We fell like shedding leaves
Spiralling down
spinning helplessly
Unable to hold on what
once was
we crashed onto the ground
from blooming flowers
we become beautiful debris.

It's unsettling how some people
Come close to you
Because of your warmth
Then they light up a match
And watch you burn
Until your soul is in ashes
And all that remains
Are little embers fading into dust
Then they tell you
It was your fault all along.

Till the End

She paints her sorrows
with metaphors and word collages
each stroke spells her heartbreaks well
and her eyes are floodgates
with tears free-falling
drenching her soul's week outer shell

There is a dew on
the grass,
unfathomable Sybille
tears;
Shuddering in the sunlight
each one will be
obliterated by the passing
of time
or the imprint
of a shoe, whichever
arrives soonest into
the circle!

Till the End

All I have left of you
are words on paper
that you walked away from
but your memory will remain
as long as there is ink in my pen

The raindrops talk about me
how they drizzled on a girl
drenched in tears..!

AT A DISTANCE I AM THERE

I hold the warmth of the captured moment,
in the palm of my cold hands,
though the moment is long gone
yet my hands say longer, just a little bit longer!

I was never meant to be
a trophy nor a medallion
I am not even a book or a chapter
I'm verses and syllables
I'm tears and laughter
I'm heart and soul
I'm today, tomorrow and forever after

Stay if you can make me love
my scarred soul.
Stay if you can make me embrace
my imperfections
Stay if you can say
that "you're one in a trillion"
Stay like a moon
and light up my galaxy

Will you?

Will you come around
Just to check on me
Will you show up
when I'll be in need
Will you help me out

Till the End

When every single
Scar will freeze
Will you show me the way
when everything looks chaotic
Will you stay by my side
when everything seems scary
Will you be a part of my untold story!?

Dear Future,

In this amazing world of passing

Clouds and living clouds,

I just want to tell you something.

I know we haven't met

Still, don't know who'll hold this dad's

Princess But this eye started

Longing for you to hold on!!

One day we will be known,

I will stare at your eyes

as a couple, will hold your hands

we will walk together

we will become great friends

Sharing's with non-stop laughter's

we will have an unbreakable bond

If I fall, will you catch me?

If I cry, will you hold me?

If I hurt you, will you ever forgive me?

Till the End

In my dream, I'll see you through
From dawn, I'll be waiting
Until dusk, I'll be there too
All my dreams, all my love, a life with you
Be my last heartbeat that ends with you.

God has perfect timing; never early,
Never late
It takes a little patience and faith,
but it's worth the wait.
His will, waiting with patience to hold
your hands with showers of blessings!!

Hey Zoe,

**Stop thinking that your life is meaningless,
and keep flying
Because you may not know how many
broken hearts find meaning in your colours.**

9 789355 331953